Shouting at The Void

Amanda Morrison

BookLeaf Publishing

India | USA | UK

Presentation by *BookLeaf Publishing*

Web: www.bookleafpub.com

E-mail: info@bookleafpub.com

ISBN: 9789363312029

First edition 2024

To the lonely, to the awkward, misfits, black sheeps, gypsy souls, horror junkies. To the ones who've been told you could never, to the ones afraid of failure, to the ones hurt by love..

This is for us.

PREFACE

So many demons, so little holy water.

A warning, you may feel things when you read these, the feelings may not always be sunshine and rainbows. This is life.

Tidal Wave

I have so many words that are trying to come out
all at once I can barely form a syllable.
A thousand and one thoughts raging in my head
at the same time and I am paralyzed in place by
the weight of it all.
I just sit and repeat the same old cycle like an
untreated illness, I need someone to slap some
sense into me.
It's hard to stay swimming when there is no
shore in sight.
With aching muscles I push through the waves
even as my light seems to fade.
I want to scream at the ocean to just let me
drown, to let me just sink all the way down.
I'm tired of being strung along like a
puppet,dancing with such joy only while the
master's amusement lasts just to be placed back
on the shelf to gather dust.
I deserve more than this. I just don't know what's
wrong with me to feel like maybe I don't.
I try so fucking hard to be a life boat for
everyone in my life, yet they never seem to
notice the water that stays behind when I pull
them from the storm.

They are drowning me to save themselves and
when I cry for mercy they play the victim like a
grandiose actor in flamboyant fashion.
I am struggling with the energy to keep myself
floating in this tidal wave of despair, the life
boat has taken on too much water.
No shore still in sight and the brightness of the
stars are hiding behind ominous clouds.
I no longer know which direction I am heading
or if I should even be heading there.
All I can do is ride the wave and see what
happens when I get there. One of two things is
going to happen. One, I find what I'm looking
for and can let the sun kiss away this melancholy
that weighs my soul down.
Two, I drift aimlessly waiting for the final storm
that finally sinks me to the bottom.

Bottled

There is an eternal tug of war threatening to rip my soul in half. I just want to be heard yet I feel I just bother people and say nothing. I just continue to bottle my emotions, I feel like a distillery. I put on my best fake smile for the public to see yet inside my head I'm wishing I would just get hit by a bus. The fact I can make people believe that I'm actually fine makes me wonder if they ever really knew me at all. Please keep your sympathies, I have no use for pity. I'm tired of staying alive out of spite but not as tired then I am of hiding it. There are so many times I stare in the mirror and just want to punch the reflection until my knuckles are bloody. I give and give and give some more until I can't give anymore just to be thrown away because I stopped giving. I want to be seen but I'm afraid of scaring people away with these demons that keep me awake. My soul is tired of this tug of war, it's ripping at the seams. I'm finding it harder to stitch it back together, running out of string. I'm afraid if I don't pour out this bottle that the glass will shatter completely. You can feel the hairline fractures forming from the pressure. I start to drink from my own misery

hoping the bottle will hold on for a while longer.
Caught in a vicious cycle of emptying and
filling, longing for someone to share a drink.

Rat Race

5

When you have a four lane highway and six
lanes worth of traffic rushing through your head
it's hard to keep track of all the cars. Some are
speeding cars that distract you with their bright
colors zipping past you as they weave in and out
of the mess.
You have your old beaters that seem to never
die, holding up traffic by going too slow in the
fast lane.
Let us not forget the ones who are honking their
horns when things get jammed up, the ones that
make a bad situation worse.
Too many cars and not enough lanes
What am I to do?
I try to keep the cars moving the best that I can
but the beaters are blocking up traffic and the
horns are getting louder.
Hey, did you see that car?! Man that thing was
fast.
Oh right now what was I saying? I seemed to
have lost my place.
Oh well here we go another day of the rat race

Appetizer

I've been told I feel too much, too quickly, too loudly and maybe that's true, however I have terrible news. I give two shits less. If my intensity intimidates you, then it is you who are too weak. You get what you get, and when I give boy do I give. You can either deal with it or you can walk away. It's as simple as it sounds. I'm so tired of trying to water myself down for others. You can go ahead and choke from now on. You can keep choking until you learn to chew. I am not intended as an appetizer, I'm the whole entree.

Tired

I'm not tired of being alone, I'm tired of feeling lonely. Tired of only having the voices in my head for conversation. Always the one checking on others and taking care of their needs yet I have to do everything for myself by myself. I'm spread so thin that I forget to eat for days in a row to the point my body is dwindling in size by the day yet I make sure everyone else eats. I'm literally wasting away and long as I say I'm fine people don't ask. I just want to scream at them, no I'm not ok, my soul feels like it's a thousand pounds and I'm oh so very tired of carrying the weight. Just because I've carried this weight alone most of life doesn't mean I should've ever had to. I'm no longer strong but stuck in position keeping the weight from crushing me completely.

Choke

Sometimes I shove my foot in my mouth
And choke on the words I want to shout
Rambling in circles like a hamster in a wheel
Bleeding from the wounds that refuse to heal
My blood drips on the pages as I write
Bittersweet words that belong to the night
Pain is like the rain and I'm just a cloud
I hold it all in til it comes falling down
It washes away my senses,numbs how I feel
It blurs together the imaginary and the real
I can't seem to keep my thoughts straight
Feeling stuck outside of Hell's gates

Fantasy

I find my fingers tracing the edges of you when I
see you smiling in a photograph. I wish it was
your warm skin that I felt wrapped around mine,
the edges of our bodies blurring into one. I
wonder if your lips taste as sweet as the words
they whisper to me. Your low grumbly voice
resonates in my core like ringing a bell that has
been untouched for so long. I want to feel the
hot air on my ear lobes as you call me a good
girl just to watch me squirm while you hold me
against you. I want to give you every piece of
me. I know it's just a fantasy, a figment of my
imagination, someone like you doesn't fall for
someone like me. I should just give up this silly
dream and so many times I have tried. Then I
hear hotel California on the radio on the way to
work and you're the only thought in my head.
The melody surrounds me and I daydream of
you next to me with your hand on my thigh as I
drive. I dream of you pulling me in close,
holding me tight against you as you place the
softest kiss on my forehead. I tell you how
gorgeous I think your eyes are as you try to
cover them with your hair, running my fingers
through to move it out the way as I tell you

again. I'm happy with how our friendship is, but I can't help the fact that I still have these feelings. Every time I think I know how I feel, I'm reminded that just because I decided to not act on these feelings out of respect doesn't mean that my heart chose to stop aching for you. It may always wait for the opportunity even if it knows it will never come.

Bye

Who is this coming knocking upon my door?
A handsome stranger I've never met before
A playful smile resting upon his face
Soft eyes with a touch of grace
He left fast and in a hurry
Igniting my passion and stirring my fury
Now the beast is awake and it demands to be
tamed
Waiting for the one to be memorized by the
flame

Not good enough for a long time
But great for a good time
It's fine, I understand
You don't need to explain
We all have our parts to play
I'll throw these feelings in the trash
Right where you left me

Songs & daydreams

Every song that has graced my playlist today has made me think about you. Each time a different daydream, changing in harmony to the beats. From cemetery strolls as we have deep conversations about life and death on a sunny fall day; to me dancing a fool in the kitchen as we cook a meal together trying to make you laugh. From watching our favorite horror movies as we cuddle on the couch to surprising you with lunch while you're busy working as I massage your shoulders planting soft kisses on the top of your head. The music may change and the particulars of the wants may change however it seems that you are the constant. I want to hold you, to touch you, caresse you, kiss you. YOU, that's the important word that drives me insane. I don't want someone like you or someone who treats me similar to you, I want you. Funny isn't it? Wanting the things we know we can't have. I'll just have to enjoy the daydreams for what they are, the dreams of a thawing heart. You're probably questioning every word that you're reading right now wondering how I could possibly feel this way. The truth is, I don't have an answer. It's not something so simply put into words, poets have been trying for centuries.

Opposites

14

I want to go left but my brain says right
Society says work my heart says write
I say hello and they say goodbye
Leaving me soon as I arrive
Living in a world of opposites
Told we're negative when we're being positive
They stopped listening and we stopped talking
We're busy running while they're in the way
walking

What a shame

15

Are you really complaining again? You act like you're always the victim, reminds me of a toddler having a tantrum. How is it that you get to complain and bring your shitty mood on my doorstep while I respectfully let you have your feelings but if I finally feel like I'm drowning and vent you somehow make it about yourself, trying to give me advice as if you possibly understand. You don't have the responsibilities that I do or the stress that comes with it. You think because you tell me you care and that you love me that I'm going to not notice how you have nothing to say unless you need money or you want to bitch about your parents, I wish I could bitch about my parents. I tell you about my best friend and because it's a guy you acted jealous and tried to hide it in humor as if I was some kind of idiot. You half ass support my dreams and have the audacity to criticize his support instead of stepping your game up. What a shame.

Big easy vibes

The neon lights of the big easy shine in my soul like technicolor memories, mixed with the ambient flicker of the streetlamps. The ones that used to mean you better be home by then. The sweet smell of jasmine in the evening and the sweet taste of iced taste in the hot afternoon. The smell of amazing food always teases your stomach like a lover would. We can go Cajun dancing along the river or find a jazz club from the old days. You never have to go far to find a party, usually one finds you. Street performers and thrown together bands are a staple of the French quarter. New Orleans is more than just my home, it's a part of my soul. You don't just travel there, you experience it. When you leave it stays with you. Maybe as a new favorite food or maybe you start to tell everyone you see hello. There's a reason we're called the big easy, we take life easy and we roll with the times. Life is short might as well live it up.

Lovesick in the friendzone

My heart suddenly skips a beat
Whenever our hands accidentally meet
We always seem to pull them away
Afraid of the consequences if they stayed
The ice in our veins may hopelessly thaw
The walls we built could crumble and fall
We pretend that it didn't happen
Starting conversation to breed distraction
Then our eyes meet too long in a stare
Forgetting that anyone else is there
You're stuck in my head like a catchy song
Making me feel like I finally belong
Looking away to hide our blushing faces
My heart doesn't beat, it stammers and races
It sings a beautiful song and only I hear it
I want to put your hand on my heart so you can
feel it
Palms starting to sweat and getting nervous
Wishing I could convince you we deserve this
I try to speak but no words come to my aid
I'm not scared of much but of this I'm afraid
I can hear you in my head like a gentle scream
Somebody pinch me this must be a dream
My ears long to hear you call my name
No matter the time these feelings remain

They can not drown they seem to float
Fighting on in the name of hope
Maybe one day we won't pull away
And these can be more than just words I say
I'll have you anyway I can in the end
Whether it be lovers or best of friends

Reminder

I take my job as a friend very seriously. I shower the ones I love with support like a gardener watering plants to watch the flowers bloom. I'm an open ear when they need to vent and I pay attention when they say nothing at all. I'm quick with a joke when they need one or just to hear them laugh. I hug them tight when I haven't seen them in a while and I always wait until my friends make it in the house before leaving. I believe in effort, the be safe and have a good day texts and letting people know when I see things that make me think about them. Knowing someone cares and being reminded are two different things. This is your reminder.

PSA

This is a Public Service Announcement, does anybody know what exactly the fuck? Is this just one long Greek tragedy that is being dragged out by bad acting? We keep waiting for the final bow but they keep monologuing and the audience is bored to tears. Asking for people to respect your right to live should not be a question. Live how you want, love who you want. Human rights should never be based upon anything other than being alive.

Sensory overload

21

The lights are too bright and the sounds are too loud. My clothes are too tight and I can feel gravity pushing me into the ground. All at once like a ill timed parade of clashing cultures. Confusion circling me as would a hungry vulture. I grind my teeth and bounce my leg as I try to process the overload. A hug from the right person would melt away my senses and free my heart. Just the thought can calm the ocean tide that swells inside. Be warned the waters may still be turbulent even if the sun peaks out between the clouds. The storm will pass and the ocean will settle. Unload your senses and take a deep breath. Remind yourself you're doing your best.

Connection through radio

I cranked the radio up as loud as it would go,
Hotel California was on again. I sing out loud
with confidence that I don't usually possess for I
always see it as a sign that the universe is
connecting us for those moments. A few minutes
to feel not alone even if it's just in my head.
Sometimes that is where we are the most lonely.
I smile as I sway to the guitar solo. The song
ends and I must go on about my errands a little
lighter then I was before. On the return trip
home of all things I hear Ghost on the radio and
I laugh out loud to the universe, the band I only
tried listening to because he said I would like it
and he wasn't wrong. What is the coincidence of
two separate songs that both connect me to you
would play on separate radio stations so
perfectly timed with my driving. It's almost as if
the universe wanted you to go grocery shopping
with me.

When the void whispers back

I can no longer contain this rage that's burning
inside
This time I'll scream instead of a silent sigh
You don't get to tell me how to live my life
anymore
That ended when you walked out that door
You don't get to bring misery upon me and tell
me to smile
That's not how emotions work not by a mile
You better watch that condescending tone when
you speak
Just because I'm nice doesn't mean I'm weak
I scream into the void until my voice cracks in
pain
So much energy lost and none to be gained
I could break down and cry but what good
would that do?
Like hiring a poacher to work at a zoo
I'll let out what I have to and move on with a
lighter sack
Sometimes when you scream into the void, it
whispers back.

Hopeless romantic

I'm just a hopeless romantic at heart. I want to hold your thigh while we're driving around singing along badly to the radio. I'm the look at the moon type of girl who wants to slow dance in the kitchen at 2 in the morning. I cherish staying up until the birds start to chirp talking and listening with no stone left unturned. I call myself a hopeless romantic when really I am just a romantic who is hopeless. So few have value in old fashioned romance such as writing love letters for your partner to find when you're not around. I give with my whole being and I can't seem to give enough. Just a hopeless romantic in a world with little love.

Gain

What goes up must come down
But what goes down eventually comes back up
You might have to dig
You might have to crawl
But you can never fly
If you don't first fall
So pull yourself together and dust the dirt off
This was just a yield not a pit stop
Roll with the punches and smile through the
pain
You have nothing to lose and everything to gain

Thank you

Thank you for giving my words a home
For giving meaning to what I thought was gone
Thank you for pushing me to better myself
I only hope to return the favor
Thank you for seeing me when I felt unseen
I'll cherish that forever
Thank you for not leaving when you had the
chance
My soul owes yours a dance